DIGITAL AND INFORMATION LITERACY ™

GAMING
PLAYING SAFE AND PLAYING SMART

COLIN WILKINSON

rosen publishing's
rosen central®

New York

Dedicated to Chris, Nick, Andi, and my brother Evan, for keeping my kill counts high and my trigger finger exercised

Published in 2012 by The Rosen Publishing Group, Inc.
29 East 21st Street, New York, NY 10010

First Edition

Library of Congress Cataloging-in-Publication Data

Wilkinson, Colin, 1977–
Gaming: playing safe and playing smart/Colin Wilkinson.—1st ed.
    p. cm.—(Digital and information literacy)
Includes bibliographical references and index.
ISBN 978-1-4488-5552-0 (library binding)—
ISBN 978-1-4488-5611-4 (pbk.)—
ISBN 978-1-4488-5612-1 (6-pack)
1. Internet games—Juvenile literature. 2. Internet—Safety measures—Juvenile literature. 3. Computer games—Juvenile literature. 4. Video games—Juvenile literature. I. Title.
GV1469.15.W55 2012
794.8—dc23

2011019967

Manufactured in the United States of America

CPSIA Compliance Information: Batch #W12YA: For further information, contact Rosen Publishing, New York, New York, at 1-800-237-9932.

CONTENTS

INTRODUCTION

Over the past thirty years, video games have become one of the fastest-growing and most popular forms of home entertainment. After making the jump from the arcade to the living room, video game consoles have continued to grow in power and possibilities, adapting to and creating new technologies at a rapid pace. Using today's faster and smaller hardware, players can receive close to the same level of visual quality and depth of interaction on a portable device as on a dedicated gaming computer or console.

With the Internet's increasing incorporation into games, players have found new venues for virtual socializing within deeply engaging fantasy realms. Today's games allow players to interact directly with one another regardless of their location. This coming together through gaming helps knock down traditional barriers to communication, such as sex, ethnicity, nationality, race, and age. The competitive nature of games can kindle enduring friendships or create long-standing but friendly rivalries as players bond within a guild or as part of a team.

Even now, new genres of games to play—and new ways to play them—are being developed. Motion tracking and 3-D allow players to control a game within real spaces—an idea that not too long ago belonged

Video games are big business. Each year, new trends and upcoming releases at conventions, such as the Consumer Electronics Show, are carefully watched by the media, the gaming industry, and eagerly awaiting fans.

only within the realm of science fiction. Expanding gameplay with live audio or video chat, friend status, rewards tracking, and updated downloadable content keeps players invested in the games for longer periods of time than in the past.

With nearly three-quarters of Americans devoting time each day to enjoy video games, learning the safe way to play has become a necessity. Dangers inherent within gaming have become a reality. Physical ailments caused by repetitive motion or poor posture over long periods of time can have a negative lifelong impact. Raised stress levels and sedentary behavior associated with games can lead to obesity. Social isolation, depression, and addiction associated with games have even been linked to death in some cases. Gaming in a healthy way by playing age-appropriate games for reasonable amounts of time is not only smart, but it will also make playing video games even more fun.

Chapter 1

From *Tennis for Two* to Massively Multiplayer Online Role-Playing Games:
A Brief History of Video and Computer Games

The video game's humble beginnings can be traced to 1958, when *Tennis for Two*—the first game of its kind and the predecessor of the extremely popular *Pong*—ran on an analog computer using a primitive oscilloscope display. Today, the multimillion-dollar video game industry features titles that run on highly complex and powerful home gaming consoles.

The world of video games has experienced massive growth in popularity and has become a force to be reckoned with in the entertainment industry. In fact, in recent years more time and money have been spent on video and computer games than on watching, buying, or renting movies.

Rudimentary by today's standards, early games such as *Pong* still provide a fun gaming experience, as demonstrated by these two players at the Computer Game Museum in Berlin, Germany.

Games have come a long way from the coin-op arcades of the 1970s and '80s, but many of today's games—including popular genres such as puzzle games, platformers, fighting games, and even first-person shooters—trace their roots back to the arcades of yesteryear.

Gaming Goes Home

By the mid-1970s, video game companies, seeking to open up a new revenue stream and boost profits, were looking to expand beyond arcades into homes. The first home gaming console was the Magnavox Odyssey, released in 1972. This system included several built-in games and used printed plastic sheets, which were placed on the television to define the game field. In the mid-1970s, students and hobbyists created the first role-playing games, often as text-only adventure games. These early efforts spurred the inception of notable game development companies, including Infocom and Stormfront.

By the early 1980s, home gaming systems had expanded to include the Atari 2600, ColecoVision, and Intellivision. These new systems featured swappable game cartridges that allowed for more games to be created, sold, and played. Although primitive compared to today's gaming consoles, the faster processing power and greatly improved graphics capability of these early systems captured the eager attention of millions of consumers who greatly enjoyed the home playing experience.

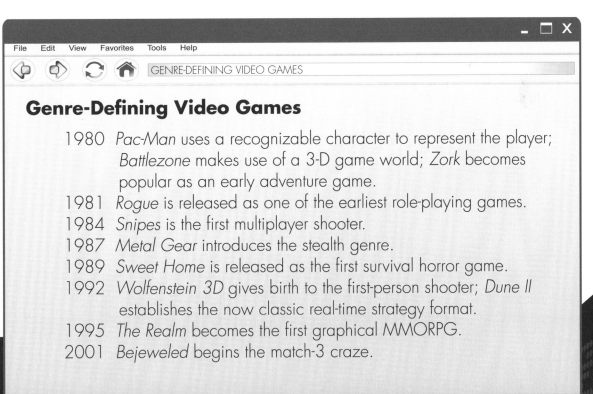

File   Edit   View   Favorites   Tools   Help

GENRE-DEFINING VIDEO GAMES

Genre-Defining Video Games

1980   *Pac-Man* uses a recognizable character to represent the player; *Battlezone* makes use of a 3-D game world; *Zork* becomes popular as an early adventure game.
1981   *Rogue* is released as one of the earliest role-playing games.
1984   *Snipes* is the first multiplayer shooter.
1987   *Metal Gear* introduces the stealth genre.
1989   *Sweet Home* is released as the first survival horror game.
1992   *Wolfenstein 3D* gives birth to the first-person shooter; *Dune II* establishes the now classic real-time strategy format.
1995   *The Realm* becomes the first graphical MMORPG.
2001   *Bejeweled* begins the match-3 craze.

Stronger, Smaller, Sharper, Faster

In the mid-1980s, game systems had advanced even further to include improved power-utilizing components dedicated to specific tasks and multi-function controllers with new forms of input. The prime example of this was the Nintendo Entertainment System, which was released in 1985.

Home gaming technology continued to advance. By the early 1990s, computers and video game consoles began to feature higher-resolution graphics, full 3-D, and online components, making for a far more engaging gaming experience. With this wider range of technical capabilities came

Handheld systems, such as this portable version of Nintendo's *Mario Bros.*, brought games out of the arcades and living rooms and helped pave the way for today's popular casual and mobile games.

a corresponding broadening of creative options. As a result, the 1990s saw the emergence of many genre-defining games. These included survival horror, real-time strategy, adventure, simulation, and first-person shooter games.

Gaming hardware in the 1990s didn't just become faster. It also became smaller, as handheld gaming systems, including the Nintendo Game Boy, Sega Game Gear, and Atari Lynx, began to appear. The success of these platforms led to a new style of games suited to quick bursts of play, eventually feeding into what has become the casual and mobile gaming market.

More powerful gaming systems with a larger install base help create new possibilities in game genres, such as popular music games involving elaborate controllers and add-ons.

Since the 1990s, the home gaming market has been dominated primarily by the so-called Big Three: Nintendo, Sony, and Microsoft, the latter having entered the gaming market in 2001. The heightened power of today's systems allow for more realistic—or artfully stylized—3-D graphics, immersive audio, complex artificial intelligence (AI) behaviors, and dynamic story progression.

Recent years have seen the rollout of even more innovations, including the rise of the music genre, spearheaded by games like *Guitar Hero* and *Rock Band*; the introduction of motion controls on the Nintendo Wii and, later, the PlayStation Move and Xbox Kinect; and the saturation of online gaming across nearly all genres and gaming systems.

Home gaming consoles are forever increasing in power. For this reason, technologies once foreign to the home—such as 3-D, HD, and touch control—as well as new styles of play and game genres will continue to be created and defined based on the latest and still-emerging cutting-edge technologies.

Chapter 2

Genres and Their Ratings

There are many genres of video games and a wide variety of audiences that they are designed for. Not all video games are suitable for or designed to be played by children or even teens. They have adult content, including extreme violence, that is equivalent to that found in R-rated movies. Some video game genres tend to gravitate toward certain types of adult content and frequently receive restrictive ratings. For instance, first-person shooters tend to be violent by nature. This is signaled even in the genre's title. Their content and suitability for young players have become a major subject of debate among state and federal lawmakers.

It is essential to understand and follow the ratings guidelines whenever you are shopping for and playing games to guarantee that you are not being exposed to content that is not designed specifically for your age group.

Why Games Are Rated

Game ratings in the United States have been applied since the mid-1990s. The introduction of these ratings was originally in response to controversy

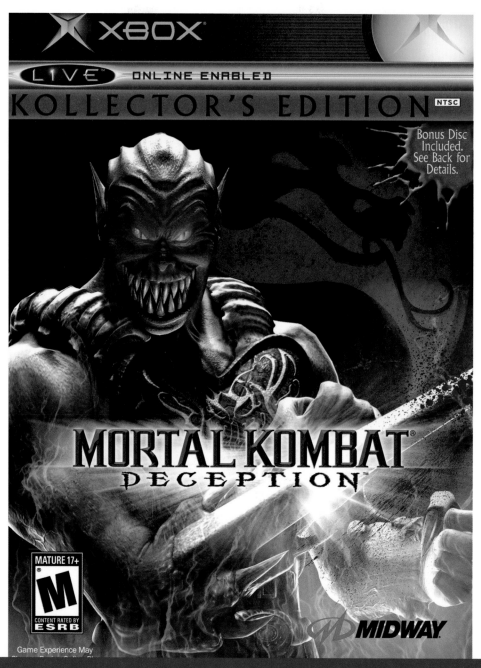

XBOX

LIVE ONLINE ENABLED

KOLLECTOR'S EDITION NTSC

Bonus Disc
Included.
See Back for
Details.

MORTAL KOMBAT®
DECEPTION™

MATURE 17+
M
CONTENT RATED BY
ESRB

Game Experience May

MIDWAY

Mortal Kombat helped inspire the creation of a formal video games rating process to inform gamers and parents about the type of content included within games and its age appropriateness.

that had sprung up around violent video games, including *Mortal Kombat* and *Doom*. These games took advantage of new high-powered graphics hardware to include more realistic depictions of violence than previously possible.

Concerns over young people's exposure to this graphic and extreme violence led to legal hearings beginning in 1992. The result was the creation of the Entertainment Software Rating Board (ESRB) in 1994. The ESRB and similar organizations worldwide are responsible for assigning ratings to video games, enforcing advertising guidelines related to video game sales, and helping ensure responsible online privacy practices. The ratings process is not mandatory. However, since many stores refuse to sell unrated games, the ESRB rating is now applied to almost all games. A game's rating is displayed on the front of its packaging, and a more descriptive explanation for the rating can be found on the back.

Action and Adventure Games

Action titles encompass a wide range of games and may include platformer games such as the youth-friendly *Super Mario Bros.* or *Ratchet and Clank*. They also include more violent first-person shooters like *Call of Duty*. Echoing this range in content, applicable ratings are equally diverse.

First-person shooters embed the player in game scenarios so that he or she becomes the in-game character. This heightens the experience and thrill of gameplay, in part by making the player's in-game decisions more personal. Recent studies have shown that middle school students who play violent video games, especially first-person shooters, tend to become more verbally and physically aggressive and take less interest in helping their peers. The long-term impact of these games, with their highly authentic, real-world scenarios and realistic depictions of extreme violence, can be devastating to players unprepared or unequipped for such graphic realism. For these reasons, many first-person shooter games have become rated M—for mature audiences only—and this rating should not be taken lightly.

Stores selling video games are responsible for informing consumers about game ratings and enforcing these ratings by not selling games rated as mature to underage buyers. Sellers may ask for proper identification for mature-rated titles.

On the opposite end of the spectrum, many action and adventure games are rated E (for everyone) or E10+ (for everyone ten and older). These general-audience, youth-friendly games provide a suitable challenge and fun gameplay for young people and their families. They tend not to delve into overly serious, dark, violent, or otherwise graphic content.

Arcade Games

Arcade titles, including retro games and fighters, offer exciting gameplay. They are easy for beginners to pick up and begin playing, while also providing additional depth and strategy for those who are more experienced. Due to the accessible nature of these games, many of them are rated for a wide audience. Yet some of the more violent fighting games receive ratings for more mature audiences.

Strategy Games

Strategy games come in many forms and include digital versions of card games, board games, and puzzle games, as well as popular real-time or turn-based strategy games. Many of these games are suitable for most audiences. However, these games can often be used as a means for gambling or may include actual gambling elements, such as in a poker game. The ESRB uses "Simulated Gambling" and "Real Gambling" descriptors to help identify these elements. The presence of gambling elements often affects the rating assigned to the game, making it unsuitable for younger players.

Sports Games

Sports titles, due to their broad appeal and need to be accessible to fans of all ages of the games' real-world counterpart, tend to be developed with an E or E10+ rating in mind. Unless the sport itself is overly violent, or the game presents a unique spin on it involving more mature story elements or

The popularity of sports games ensures that they are always early adapters of new technology, such as the motion controls available on the Nintendo Wii.

enhanced violence, sports games receive ratings that make them ideal to play with friends and family members of all ages.

Educational Games

Educational games are not a genre in and of themselves. In fact, they can be found within all the genres previously mentioned, including strategy games, arcade games, and even first-person shooters.

Many games not originally intended as educational games have proved to be great learning tools for science, history, math, and social studies, among other subjects. Games like *Oregon Trail* and *Sid Meier's Civilization* are even used to teach history in the classroom using fun and interactive means. More recent, seemingly abstract puzzle games such as *Everyday Genius: SquareLogic* and *SpaceChem* teach math, chemistry, and logic skills without ever losing the feel of a game. Research has even shown that MMORPGs, including *World of Warcraft*, can improve the reading, planning, social, and leadership skills so highly valued in the "real world."

File   Edit   View   Favorites   Tools   Help

HOW A VIDEO GAME CONSOLE WORKS

How a Video Game Console Works

- The game software, stored on disk or cartridge, maintains the instructions and art and audio assets specific to the game.
- Input devices, such as controllers or microphones, translate the player's commands to the system.
- The system's central processing units (CPUs) interpret the game and controller instructions to provide gameplay results.
- The logic board communicates the game data to and from each component.
- Memory is used to store game information and assets for quick access, either temporarily in RAM or more permanently on a hard drive or flash drive.
- Dedicated components are responsible for displaying the game's graphics, playing the game's audio, and communicating with the Internet.
- The console's operating system is responsible for handling standard instructions, such as loading or stopping a game. It often includes a graphical interface for the player.

Recent and New Game Genres

In recent years, the growth of Internet-based gaming and the development of new technology have spurred the rise of several fresh and innovative video game genres. With nearly 80 percent of the American population using the Internet on a regular basis, online video games and MMORPGs have earned a devoted following. The popular online game *World of Warcraft* has close to twelve million players worldwide, and many recent games feature online multiplayer modes as major features within the game.

With online content driven, at least in part, by the players of the game, it is difficult to accurately rate online games. It is not uncommon to see a

Multiplayer gaming places an emphasis on the social aspects of play, often by utilizing cooperative, rather than competitive and adversarial, gaming possibilities.

notice alongside the ESRB rating stating that "Online Interactions Not Rated by the ESRB." This lack of clarity from the ratings board, though understandable, makes online gaming difficult territory to navigate for players seeking an age-appropriate experience. The task is made easier, however, by many game designers. They often provide in-game options allowing users to disable certain features, such as chat and user-generated content, that may skew a game toward more adult content.

With the introduction of the Nintendo Wii in 2006, and more recently the Sony Move and Microsoft Kinect, motion gaming has players engaging in interactive media like never before. Most games for the systems have been designed for a broad audience and family-friendly play. As such, most motion-based games are suitable for all ages and carry ratings of E or E10+.

Also of particular note are mobile and social games—two of the fastest-growing video game platforms designed for mobile devices and smartphones. Neither of these types of games receives ratings from the ESRB. Apple's iTunes Store and the Android Market both feature content ratings by age group for such games, but these do not correspond closely with the ESRB ratings. In addition, mobile and social games do not receive the same careful degree of scrutiny that video and computer games reviewed by the ESRB do. Many Web and social games, such as games available on the popular social networking site Facebook, are often not rated for content appropriateness at all.

Chapter 3

Gaming and a Balanced, Healthy Life

Video games have become a major source of entertainment in the lives of North Americans of all ages. A recent study has shown that approximately 70 percent of all Americans play video games on a regular basis. With so much gaming going on, other recreational activities have declined. For instance, on average, Americans now spend more time playing video games than watching movies. It's good to be aware of the trade-offs one must make in order to find time for gaming. It is important for gamers to seek and maintain a healthy balance between gaming and other beneficial activities.

Real-world Dangers in Virtual World Play

Video games can provide a lot of benefits to the player, including boosting one's logical and critical thinking skills, improving hand-eye coordination, and enhancing multitasking abilities. Unfortunately, gaming can also have some serious negative side effects when pursued to excess. Similar to the

The allure of the elements of escapism offered by video games, when not kept in check with proper time management, can lead to gaming addiction and dependence.

various components of a healthy diet that must be balanced and moderated, playing video games can represent only one aspect of a healthy lifestyle. It can't be an entire lifestyle unto itself. Studies have shown that excessive playing of video games can lead to obesity, seizures, and physical disorders associated with repetitive motions. These can include carpal tunnel syndrome and tendonitis. All of these conditions have long-term consequences and affect routine activities other than playing games.

It has also been established that playing games excessively may increase depression and anxiety levels and lead to gaming addiction, particularly in youths. Extreme cases of video game addiction have even lead to suicide and death by self-neglect. Violent video games have also been shown to negatively affect behavior, making players more aggressive in general.

When too much time is spent playing games, other areas of life are neglected. School grades may drop. Players may become socially isolated. Their bodies may become sedentary. Other interests and hobbies may be abandoned, and creativity and imaginative thinking often goes undeveloped. When playing games featuring age-inappropriate content, bad habits such as vulgar language and aggressive, antisocial behavior may be picked up. In more extreme cases, players may even develop problems distinguishing reality from fantasy.

Be on the Alert

In order to regulate the time spent playing video games, be aware of what is being played, when it's being played, and for how long. Don't just start playing and continue until you get bored or are interrupted. Otherwise, many hours may go by before you stop playing. Set a maximum amount of time you will allow yourself for playing games each day, and stick to this limit. Some games and consoles feature timers that help users regulate the time they spend playing. Be diligent about quitting when time is up, and learn to save exciting gameplay for the next gaming session. Learning to use these tools can be an invaluable help in creating a balanced life, one in which gaming doesn't come to occupy a disproportionate place among your other important activities, interests, and responsibilities.

Stay Active

In order to combat repetitive stress syndrome, obesity tied to sedentary behavior, and other physical ailments typical of excessive gaming, it is important to exercise regularly. When gaming, this translates to taking frequent breaks. It is recommended that gamers take a ten-minute break every hour while playing. Simply moving around, stretching, and giving your eyes a rest from the television or monitor can provide a big boost for the body

Taking regular breaks during video game sessions will help avoid unhealthy stress on one's eyes and muscles. Such stress can lead to temporary ailments, like headaches, as well as more serious and long-term concerns, like repetitive stress disorder.

and will help reduce the risks of video game addiction. This is especially important when playing motion-controlled games, which can be physically demanding. Properly stretch before, during, and after play sessions.

Although playing games may not seem like a physical activity, games can often be stress-inducing and taxing to the brain. A gamer's brain works hard to solve puzzles, explore maze-like dungeons, and respond quickly to real-time scenarios in the game world. Maintaining a healthy and regular diet—full of fruits, vegetables, and lean proteins, not just soda and snacks—will help keep the body and mind engaged, alert, and injury-free. Taking breaks for meals and nutritious snacks can even give you an edge over the competition.

In addition to taking breaks during play sessions, making proper use of the game space is crucial. Sitting too close or too far from the television will place stress on the eyes, which can result in fatigue, headaches, and permanent vision problems. Exercising the eyes by rolling them in a circle in both directions and allowing them time to focus on objects at different distances (near distance, middle distance, far distance) will help reduce eye fatigue. When playing video games, sit in a natural, comfortable position. Avoid placing stress on the back or neck and putting too much weight on any one body part, such as leaning on an elbow for support. Changing position from time to time will help reduce stress placed on any given group of muscles.

Stay Social

Just like team sports and group activities in the real world, group-oriented video games are often more fun, lively, rewarding, and productive. Playing games online, or even in the same room, with friends builds a shared experience and improves social skills. Learning to strategize new plans and communicate those plans with others allows game players to develop team-building skills often neglected in today's digital world. As powerful as artificial intelligence and non-player character behaviors have become in the gaming world, they are no replacement for playing with real people.

File   Edit   View   Favorites   Tools   Help

GAMING BENEFITS

Gaming Benefits

Video games are great fun to play, but they've also proven to be beneficial in many unforeseen ways. Some of these benefits include:

- Games can improve social skills and help children suffering from attention deficit disorders.
- Games have proven extremely useful for training purposes in a variety of settings.
- Games are used as part of physical therapy for patients to regain or improve motor skills.
- Games can improve the player's math and language skills, problem solving, and decision making.
- Games have been shown to provide children with increased self-confidence.

When not playing, it's natural to want to share and discuss one's gaming accomplishments and experiences. Playing with friends provides a natural outlet for this discussion. Creating a shared experience and developing a gaming narrative with other players can improve the act of gaming itself. It can turn more passive video game playing into a dynamic creative activity.

Know When to Walk Away

As with any other activities in life, it's important to know one's strengths and limitations and to push oneself to try new techniques and learn new skills. But don't overdo it. Video games are developed for a very broad set of players. They can never be tailored for each and every gamer. If a game becomes too frustrating or begins to no longer feel fun, stop playing. Remember, games are meant to be fun.

Often, stepping away from a game allows the mind to develop new strategies. Taking a break frees the brain from the immediate and nerve-jangling pressures exerted by the game's relentless and overstimulating audiovisual input. Chances are, returning to the game after a day or two of rest and reflection will yield better results. If a game continues to create frustration, try adjusting the level of difficulty, ask a friend to help out, or simply move on to something else. There are millions of video games out there waiting to be played; don't get hung up on only one.

Expand Your Horizons

Maintaining a healthy relationship with video gaming means not disregarding other interests, activities, and responsibilities in your life. Playing video games can help develop many skills, but it can not possibly supply everything you kneed to learn, know, experience, and share.

Make time to play a musical instrument, create a piece of art, or write a story. Playing *Guitar Hero* is not a replacement for playing a real guitar, just like playing motion-controlled active games does not provide the same exercise gained by playing sports or running around outside. Having hobbies outside of gaming will help lead to a balanced life. If it seems that there isn't enough time for other activities or that interests outside of video games are becoming neglected, it's a sure signal that you need to reduce the time spent playing games.

MYTHS & FACTS

MYTH Video games lead to violent behavior in children.

FACT Studies show that most people who commit violent crimes actually spend less time absorbing media, including video games, than the average person. Additionally, crime in the United States has dropped to an all-time low over the past thirty years, a period of time that has coincided with the emergence of video games and the growth of their widespread popularity.

MYTH Gamers become socially isolated.

FACT While there is always a possibility of isolation among single-player gamers, more games are now being designed to include social aspects. Studies show that approximately one-third of gamers play games with other family members.

MYTH Video games can make players desensitized to physical and emotional violence.

FACT It's been shown that the importance of play in all its forms (make believe, board and video games, skits, role playing, simulations, storytelling, reading books, watching movies, etc.) is an important part of human development. Games and stories allow for the exploring of emotional and physical reactions within a safe environment. Games allow players to make choices unavailable or unwanted in real life and experience the negative consequences safely. They also allow people to experiment with trial and error, make poor decisions, learn from them, correct their errors, and improve their decision making—all in a low-stakes environment.

Chapter 4

Staying Safe While Gaming

Many of today's games allow players to interact and communicate with each other online, regardless of location. The games and consoles do what they can to protect users' security and safety. Yet there is always a risk when a player is playing with people he or she does not personally know or in a more public venue such as on Facebook. Today's online gamers are often faced with annoyances and threats. These range from from lewd content and abusive players to more serious matters, such as identity theft and cyberstalking.

Online Chat

Real-time voice communication can be a crucial factor when playing team-based or co-op (cooperative) games. It allows players to alert one another to the enemy and quickly adjust their strategies. It can even enhance single-player gameplay—gone are the days of waiting to see a friend in person to relay the latest in-game discovery or brag about a new high score. Thanks to

Real-time voice chat is popular in many of today's video games. While it can heighten the play experience, it may also increase the risk of disruptive gaming behavior, including poor gaming etiquette, verbal taunting, and bullying.

Voice over Internet Protocol (VoIP), today's consoles offer a variety of options for real-time voice chat, voice memos, text messaging, and even video chat. Whether in-game or out-of-game, proper use of video game chat communication is as essential as proper cell phone etiquette.

Using voice chat while playing a game can be a great experience. As with cell phone conversations, however, the experience is best when not shared with everyone around you. Paying attention to your volume level is essential when there are others nearby and for your fellow players. It's easy to get excited about a game, but shouting into the microphone will only disrupt and upset other players. When using speakers to listen to teammates, be aware that everything that's said in-game can be overheard by others in the room, which can be distracting. To avoid confusion, learn to use the mute button on the headset or controller to keep real-life conversations out of the game.

When sending messages to friends, remember that they are often busy playing games themselves or may be away from their console. Don't expect or demand an answer immediately. Similarly, when receiving messages, it's not necessary to stop your current activity in order to reply. Don't bombard another player with messages until he or she responds. This kind of spamming is no more enjoyable than receiving junk e-mail or mobile text message spam messages. When sending pictures or videos, be mindful of others. Sending inappropriate content—text, audio, video, or images—is a quick way to have a game account suspended or get permanently banned.

Cyberbullying and Cyberstalking

Cyberbullying, the act of harassing, threatening, or embarrassing another person via online communication, has unfortunately flourished within the world of online gaming. Likewise, cyberstalking has been reported among online gamers. Some players can become quite aggressive when playing online games. Their spirit of cyber-competitiveness can morph into real-life harassment. This often involves derogatory or threatening text messages and voice chats. In group settings, other players may join in the attacks, even if unaware of their harmful effect. This is known as "piling on." Both cyberbullying and cyberstalking are serious matters that can be illegal. It is important to learn to recognize and protect oneself from this kind of negative attention.

It can be difficult to differentiate a cyberbully from an ordinary player who has become overexcited, is overly eager to meet friends online, or simply isn't very nice. Typically, cyberbullying is not a onetime communication. Instead, it involves multiple threats and attacks from a specific individual or multiple individuals working together. Sometimes other players may escalate cyberbullying attacks by inviting the involvement of adult gamers as well. This can make the attacks much more dangerous.

Responsible gaming and online communication include keeping parents informed of any dangerous or suspicious activities. Disengaging oneself from a potentially negative situation can be the best way to prevent it from worsening.

The best course of action when you've become the victim of a cyberbully attack is to take five or ten minutes away from the game. Don't react or respond to the attacks, and they may stop. If not, a parent or other trusted adult, such as a teacher, should be alerted. Be aware that, because of legal implications, schools often cannot take action against cyberbullying activity, even if their students are involved. Check to see if there is a game administrator or Web master who can be alerted to the presence of a cyberbully and who may be able to revoke that person's game privileges. Muting and blocking the offending players or switching to a different game may help for the short term. However, the bully may find other ways to continue the threats and harassment.

When it becomes apparent that someone else is becoming the victim of cyberbullying, the same rules apply. Choose not to join in the taunts. Alert a parent to the activity. Complain to a game administrator or Web master. It's important to help protect your fellow gamers.

Griefing and Cheating

Griefing is a type of play that involves using a game's design and execution against other players for mean-spirited fun. The griefer's goal is to ruin what should be a fun game experience for the other players by making the game excessively difficult and frustrating. In this way, griefers play a different "meta-game" than the other players are attempting to enjoy. Becoming angry at or counterattacking the griefing players only adds to their fun and satisfaction.

Cheating players, on the other hand, find ways to abuse the game itself, taking advantage of broken features to exploit the game's design and increase their success level. This can mean earning in-game currency quickly, moving faster, or shooting more accurately. When cheats or "mods"—a modification of the game or its communications—are used in multiplayer games, they create an unfair advantage that will certainly frustrate other players who are playing by the rules.

When confronted with a griefer or a cheater, a course of action similar to that used when responding to cyberbullies works well. First, take a break from the game, and, chances are, the offending players will move on. If possible, mute or block the player(s), or move to a different server where their disruptive play will not reach you. If possible, report the player—most game services will suspend or block accounts belonging to cheating and griefing players.

Secure Transactions

Recent trends in gaming have been steering toward digital distribution, downloading games and content directly to the gaming device, rather than purchasing boxed copies from a retail store. Gaming retail giant GameStop has even shifted gears to focus primarily on selling digital downloads. While some downloads are free, the majority requires purchase via either a credit card or a prepurchased game- or console-specific currency.

Whatever currency the purchase requires, sensitive billing information is nearly always required at some point during the transaction. Whenever purchasing a new download, the credit card holder should always be present. Do not charge something to your parent's credit card without his or her permission and supervision. Even when using prepurchased points or gift cards, it's best to consult a parent before making a purchase and giving out any sensitive information.

File   Edit   View   Favorites   Tools   Help

TOOLS FOR SAFE GAMING

Tools for Safe Gaming

- Use a timer or cell phone alarm to limit game sessions.
- Use a single-ear headset and keep the volume low to avoid disturbing those around you and to remain aware of your surroundings.
- Become familiar with your console's parental controls and privacy settings.
- Use a robust password on all online gaming accounts (one that is hard for a hacker to figure out).
- Play video games in a well-lit environment to help maintain alertness and reduce eye strain.
- Plan gaming sessions with friends and family to increase the fun and safety of gaming, and to reduce time spent with disruptive players.

Sharing Information

The best guideline for playing games online is to never share personal information with anyone. This includes identifying information such as home address, what school the player attends, age, phone number, e-mail address, and real name. It's never possible to know exactly who the other players are or if they really are who they say they are. So don't give out any identifying information, even if the person you're playing and communicating with seems trustworthy.

Gamers often share information unknowingly by including it within their gaming profile or avatar information. When creating an online profile, it's best to ask for help from a parent to make sure the information made

Learning to properly manage privacy settings and friend lists can be an important step in avoiding the dangers associated with oversharing and cyberstalking.

available will not identify you to someone who might mean you harm. This will also allow a trusted adult to know exactly what information is being shared. Similarly, it is good practice to talk to a parent regularly concerning what behavior is acceptable when playing games online. Including parents in one's hobbies, such as gaming, can be a rewarding experience in itself.

Limiting Information

Today's consoles allow for players to set their own limits on sharing information and communication. They also provide tools for taking action when these limits fail or when encountering abusive players. Taking advantage of these options will help ensure a fun and safe gaming experience.

Most game systems—like Xbox, PlayStation, and Wii—allow users to take advantage of privacy controls that limit access to one's personal information to registered friends. Many also allow people to play games without having to first provide personal identifying information in a profile. Popular online and social networking venues, such as Facebook, however, often encourage players to share as much information as they are comfortable with, without ever fully disclosing who can view that information. Sharing identifying and personal information freely online can be very dangerous. It can result in cyberbullying, cyberstalking, and identity theft.

It's recommended to only post information that has been approved by a parent, and never post personal information such as a home address or phone number. Limit who can see this information, restricting it to just friends, from within the account's privacy settings. Lastly, it's best to get a parent's permission before adding new friends, even if they are schoolmates or family members.

Limiting Communication

Limits for communicating with friends and nonfriends while playing online are an option provided by most game systems. Players can often determine what groups of players can be communicated with via text, voice, and video during a game. Some systems require that players be registered friends in order to communicate via messages. This greatly reduces the chances of receiving spam or harassing messages of any sort.

Options for muting an obnoxious or abusive player are typically temporary and used during gameplay. This can usually be done by selecting from the player list view, using onscreen controls. Additional muting or blocking control varies depending on the game console. When encountering an abusive player, it's best to notify an adult. To put a quick end to the abuse, mute the player's chat, block the player from direct communication, and report the player to the system moderators. Some systems also allow players to file a complaint on a specific player by selecting the player from the player list and choosing to view the player's gamer card.

Gaming should always be safe, friendly, and above all, fun. Do your part to create a gaming environment that encourages a spirit of fair play, respect, and kindness, and notify responsible adults whenever a fellow gamer disrupts this environment. If everyone plays by the rules, there is a rich, enthralling, and hugely entertaining world of gaming to explore out there!

TEN GREAT QUESTIONS

TO ASK A VIDEO GAMES SALESCLERK

1 How long should I play games for each day?

2 How long should I play games for each week?

3 How often should I take a break during a gaming session?

4 How far from the television should I sit?

5 How can I control my privacy while playing online?

6 How can I avoid disruptive players online?

7 What console allows me the most options for security and privacy?

8 What are some of the most highly recommended games appropriate for my age?

9 What gaming accessories are available for safe and healthy gaming?

10 What options are there for online content purchases without resorting to storing a credit card on file?

GLOSSARY

console An electronic system that connects to a display (as a television set) and is used primarily to play video games.

downloadable content (DLC) A form of digital media distributed through the Internet. It can also refer to content created for video games that is released separately from the main video game release.

first-person shooter (FPS) A video game genre that centers upon gun and projectile weapon–based combat through the first-person perspective.

genre A category of artistic, musical, or literary composition characterized by a particular style, form, or content.

graphics Pictorial images displayed on a computer screen.

hardware The physical components (as electronic and electrical devices) of a computer.

innovative Characterized by, tending to, or introducing new ideas, methods, or devices.

massively multiplayer online role-playing game (MMORPG) A genre of role-playing video games in which a very large number of players interact with one another within a virtual game world.

motion control A form of game control using player movements, rather than a traditional gamepad and buttons, such as with the Wii game system.

real-time strategy (RTS) A type of strategy video game in which the action proceeds in a rapid fashion and the player must seize control of territory, assets, and resources. This style of gameplay is typical of war games.

role-playing game (RPG) A game in which players assume the roles of characters in a fictional setting.

Voice over Internet Protocol (VoIP) Technology used for live voice and multimedia communications (voice messaging, text messaging, audio and video streams, videoconferencing, etc.) sent and received via the Internet.

Educational Computing Organization of Ontario (ECOO)
10 Morrow Avenue, Suite 202
Toronto, ON M6R 2J1
Canada
(416) 489-1713
Web site: http://www.ecoo.org
The ECOO helps teachers and students incorporate computer learning into
the educational process.

Entertainment Software Association (ESA)
575 7th Street NW, Suite 300
Washington, DC 20004
Web site: http://www.theesa.com
The ESA offers a range of services to interactive entertainment
software publishers including a global antipiracy program,
business and consumer research, government relations, and
intellectual property protection efforts. The ESA also owns and
operates the E3 Expo.

Entertainment Software Rating Board (ESRB)
317 Madison Avenue, 22nd Floor
New York, NY 10017
Web site: http://www.esrb.org
The ESRB is a nonprofit, self-regulatory body established in 1994 by the
ESA. It assigns computer and video game content ratings, enforces
industry-adopted advertising guidelines, and helps ensure responsible online privacy practices for the interactive entertainment
software industry.

Family Online Safety Institute (FOSI)
815 Connecticut Avenue, Suite 220
Washington, DC, 20006
(202) 572-6252
Web site: http://www.fosi.org
The FOSI is an international, nonprofit organization that works to develop a
    safer Internet for children and families. It works to influence public
    policy and educate the public.

Get Net Wise
Internet Education Foundation
1634 I Street NW
Washington, DC 20009
Web site: http://www.getnetwise.org
Get Net Wise is part of the Internet Education Foundation, which works to
    provide a safe online environment for children and families.

Internet Keep Safe Coalition
1401 K Street NW, Suite 600
Washington, DC 20005
(866) 794-7233
Web site: http://www.ikeepsafe.org
The Internet Keep Safe Coalition is an educational resource for children and
    families that provides information on Internet safety and ethics associ-
    ated with Internet technologies.

i-SAFE Inc.
5900 Pasteur Court, Suite #100
Carlsbad, CA 92008
(760) 603-7911
Web site: http://www.isafe.org
i-SAFE is a nonprofit foundation whose mission is to educate and empower
    youth to make their Internet experiences safe and responsible. The goal is

to educate students on how to avoid dangerous, inappropriate, or unlawful online behavior.

Public Safety Canada
Attn: Public Safety Portal - SafeCanada.ca
269 Laurier Avenue
West Ottawa, ON K1A 0P8
Canada
(800) 755-7047
Web site: http://www.safecanada.ca
SafeCanada is part of the Canadian government's online efforts to make
    Canada a safe place for all its citizens wherever they are—including
    when they visit cyberspace.

Web Sites

Due to the changing nature of Internet links, Rosen Publishing has developed an online list of Web sites related to the subject of this book. This site is updated regularly. Please use this link to access the list:

http://www.rosenlinks.com/dil/game

FOR FURTHER READING

Bailey, Diane. *Cyber Ethics*. New York, NY: Rosen Central, 2008.

Bissell, Tom. *Extra Lives: Why Video Games Matter*. New York, NY: Pantheon Books, 2010.

Clark, Neils, and P. Shavaun Scott. *Game Addiction: The Experience and the Effects*. Jefferson, NC: McFarland, 2009.

Furgang, Kathy. *Netiquette: A Student's Guide to Digital Etiquette* (Digital and Information Literacy). New York, NY: Rosen Central, 2011.

Nagle, Jeanne. *Frequently Asked Questions About Wii and Video Game Injuries and Fitness*. New York, NY: Rosen Publishing, 2009.

Post Senning, Cindy. *Teen Manners: From Malls to Meals to Messaging and Beyond*. New York, NY: HarperCollins, 2007.

Sommers, Michael. *The Dangers of Online Predators*. New York, NY: Rosen Central, 2008.

Willard, Nancy. *Cyberbullying and Cyberthreats: Responding to the Challenge of Online Social Aggression, Threats, and Distress*. Champaign, IL: Research Press, 2007.

Willard, Nancy. *Cyber-Safe Kids, Cyber-Savvy Teens*. San Francisco, CA: Jossey-Bass, 2007.

Wolf, Mark J. P. *The Video Game Explosion: A History from PONG to PlayStation and Beyond*. Westport, CT: Greenwood, 2007.

Andrews, Scott F. *The Guild Leader's Handbook*. San Francisco, CA: No Starch Press, 2010.

Barab, Sasha A., and Barbara Jacobs. "Video Game Genres and Some Definitions." SimWorkshops.Stanford.edu. Retrieved March 2011 (http://simworkshops.stanford.edu/05_1007/presentations/game_genres_brutlag.pdf).

Corbett, Sara. "Learning by Playing: Video Games in the Classroom." *New York Times*, September 15, 2010. Retrieved March 2011 (http://www.nytimes.com/2010/09/19/magazine/19video-t.html).

Danielson, Richard. "Active Video Games Lead to Healthy Habits, Study Finds." *Seattle Times*, December 8, 2010. Retrieved March 2011 (http://seattle times.nwsource.com/html/health/2013616920_webgames09.html).

Dini, Kourosh. *Video Game Play and Addiction*. Bloomington, IN: iUniverse, 2008.

Donovan, Tristan. *Replay: The History of Video Games*. East Sussex, England: Yellow Ant, 2010.

ESRB and PTA. "A Parent's Guide to Video Games, Parental Controls, and Online Safety." 2008. Retrieved March 2011 (http://www.parentvideogameguide.com).

Hsu, Jeremy. "World of Warcraft Video Game Succeeds in School." Live Science, October 3, 2008. Retrieved March 2011 (http://www.livescience.com/5109-world-warcraft-video-game-succeeds-school.html).

Hunter, Nick. "Understanding Civilization (III)." Education Arcade, November 3, 2005. Retrieved February 2011 (http://www.educationarcade.org/node/66).

Internet World Stats. "Internet Usage Statistics for the Americas." Retrieved March 2011 (http://www.internetworldstats.com/stats2.htm).

Jenkins, Henry. "Reality Bytes: Eight Myths About Video Games Debunked." PBS.org. Retrieved March 2011 (http://www.pbs.org/kcts/videogamerevolution/impact/myths.html).

Kilgore, Chad. "Emotion as a Means to Prevent Griefing." Retrieved March 2011 (http://www.cs.iastate.edu/~ckilgore/portfolio/papers/An%20Exploration%20of%20Griefer%20Play.pdf).

Liptak, Adam. "Justices Debate Video Game Ban." *New York Times*, November 2, 2010. Retrieved February 2011 (http://www.nytimes.com/2010/11/03/us/03scotus.html).

Lussenhop, Jessica. "Oregon Trail: How Three Minnesotans Forged Its Path." *City Pages*, January 19, 2011. Retrieved March 2011 (http://www.citypages.com/content/printVersion/1740595).

Mackey, Robert. "Consulting American Soldiers and Yakuza Gangsters on Video Game Violence." *New York Times*, August 13, 2010. Retrieved March 2011 (http://thelede.blogs.nytimes.com/2010/08/13/consulting-american-soldiers-and-yakuza-gangsters-on-video-game-violence).

McGlothlen, John. "Violent Video Games Touted as Learning Tool." *The Gazette*, May 28, 2010. Retrieved March 2011 (http://thegazette.com/2010/05/28/violent-video-games-touted-as-learning-tool).

Rabin, Roni Caryn. "Video Games and the Depressed Teenager." *New York Times*, January 18, 2011. Retrieved February 2011 (http://well.blogs.nytimes.com/2011/01/18/video-games-and-the-depressed-teenager).

Schiesel, Seth. "Motion, Sensitive." *New York Times*, November 26, 2010. Retrieved February 2011 (http://www.nytimes.com/2010/11/28/arts/video-games/28video.html).

The Telegraph. "Internet and Video Game Safety: Ten Practical Tips to Help Protect Your Children." March 26, 2008. Retrieved February 2011 (http://www.telegraph.co.uk/news/uknews/1582862/Internet-and-video-game-safety-Ten-practical-tips-to-help-protect-your-children.html).

Vance, Patricia E. "Playing Video Games Online: The Parent-Friendly Guide." *Good Housekeeping.* Retrieved March 10, 2011 (http://www.goodhousekeeping.com/family/safety/online-video-game-safety).

Whitcomb, Daniel. "*World of Warcraft* as a Teaching Tool." WoW Insider, October 4, 2008. Retrieved February 2011 (http://wow.joystiq.com/2008/10/04/world-of-warcraft-as-a-teaching-tool).

About the Author

Colin Wilkinson is a professional video game designer, Web site designer, digital artist, and musician. He has been playing games longer than he can remember, and his favorite video game moment is reaching Kuldahar in *Icewind Dale*.

Photo Credits

Cover (background) and interior graphics © www.istockphoto.com/suprun; cover, p.1 (left to right) Jason Alden/Bloomberg via Getty Images, Nigel Treblin/AFP/Getty Images, Comstock/Thinkstock, Image Source/Getty Images; p. 5 Justin Sullivan/Getty Images; p. 8 Sean Gallup/Getty Images; p. 10 SSPL via Getty Images; p. 11 Charley Gallay/Getty Images for MTV; p. 14 Business Wire via Getty Images; p. 16 Ethan Miller/Getty Images; p. 18 Tony Avelar/Bloomberg via Getty Images; p. 20 Jason Wambsgans/Chicago Tribune/MCT via Getty Images; pp. 23, 33 Shutterstock.com; p. 25 Matthieu Spohn/PhotoAlto/Getty Images; p. 31 ColorBlind Images/Iconica/Getty Images; p. 36 J. Emilio Flores/ La Opinion/Newscom.

Designer: Nicole Russo; Photo Researcher: Amy Feinberg